AL•LEONARD
STRUMENTAL
PLAY-ALONG

FLUTE

AUDIO
ACCESS
INCLUDED

FAVORITE DISNEY SONGS

PLAYBACK+
eed • Pitch • Balance • Loop

T0066206

Audio arrangements by Peter Deneff

To access audio, visit:
www.halleonard.com/mylibrary

Enter Code
1152-2345-1452-1370

ISBN 978-1-70514-268-4

HAL•LEONARD®

Visit Hal Leonard Online at
www.halleonard.com

Contact us:
Hal Leonard
7777 West Bluemound Road
Milwaukee, WI 53213
Email: info@halleonard.com

In Europe, contact:
Hal Leonard Europe Limited
42 Wigmore Street
Marylebone, London, W1U 2RN
Email: info@halleonardeurope.com

In Australia, contact:
Hal Leonard Australia Pty. Ltd.
4 Lentara Court
Cheltenham, Victoria, 3192 Australia
Email: info@halleonard.com.au

CONTENTS

THE BALLAD OF THE LONESOME COWBOY

from TOY STORY 4

FLUTE

Music and Lyrics by
RANDY NEWMAN

EVERMORE

from BEAUTY AND THE BEAST

FLUTE

Music by ALAN MENKEN
Lyrics by TIM RICE

HOW DOES A MOMENT LAST FOREVER

from BEAUTY AND THE BEAST

FLUTE

Music by ALAN MENKEN
Lyrics by TIM RICE

HOW FAR I'LL GO

from MOANA

FLUTE

Music and Lyrics by
LIN-MANUEL MIRANDA

INTO THE UNKNOWN

from FROZEN 2

FLUTE

Music and Lyrics by KRISTEN ANDERSON-LOPEZ
and ROBERT LOPEZ

f
p
Slower
rit.
Moderately
mf
f

IT'S ALL RIGHT

featured in SOUL

FLUTE

Words and Music by
CURTIS MAYFIELD

LAVA
from LAVA

FLUTE

Music and Lyrics by
JAMES FORD MURPHY

LEAD THE WAY

from RAYA AND THE LAST DRAGON

FLUTE

Music and Lyrics by
JHENÉ AIKO

Moderately

Synth

THE PLACE WHERE LOST THINGS GO

from MARY POPPINS RETURNS

FLUTE

Music by MARC SHAIMAN
Lyrics by SCOTT WITTMAN and MARC SHAIMAN

NEVER TOO LATE
from THE LION KING 2019

FLUTE

Music by ELTON JOHN
Lyrics by TIM RICE

2
f

SPEECHLESS

from ALADDIN (2019)

FLUTE

Music by ALAN MENKEN
Lyrics by BENJ PASEK
and JUSTIN PAUL

1.
2.
f
6

TOUCH THE SKY

from BRAVE

FLUTE

Music by ALEXANDER L. MANDEL
Lyrics by ALEXANDER L. MANDEL
and MARK ANDREWS

With spirit
Fiddle and pipe

3
mf
f
Play 4 times

TRY EVERYTHING

from ZOOTOPIA

FLUTE

Words and Music by SIA FURLER,
TOR ERIK HERMANSEN and MIKKEL ERIKSEN

2.
mf
f
1.
2.
mf
f
2

YOU'RE WELCOME

from MOANA

FLUTE

Music and Lyrics by
LIN-MANUEL MIRANDA

f

REMEMBER ME

(Ernesto de la Cruz)

from COCO

FLUTE

Words and Music by KRISTEN ANDERSON-LOPEZ
and ROBERT LOPEZ